Workbook

SOCIAL STUDIES
SCOTT FORESMAN
VIRGINIA

PEARSON

Scott
Foresman

Editorial Offices: Glenview, Illinois • Parsippany, New Jersey • New York, New York
Sales Offices: Parsippany, New Jersey • Duluth, Georgia • Glenview, Illinois •
Coppell, Texas • Ontario, California

www.sfsocialstudies.com

Program Authors

Dr. Candy Dawson Boyd
Professor, School of Education
Director of Reading Programs
St. Mary's College
Moraga, California

Dr. Geneva Gay
Professor of Education
University of Washington
Seattle, Washington

Rita Geiger
Director of Social Studies and
 Foreign Languages
Norman Public Schools
Norman, Oklahoma

Dr. James B. Kracht
Associate Dean for
 Undergraduate Programs
 and Teacher Education
College of Education
Texas A & M University
College Station, Texas

Dr. Valerie Ooka Pang
Professor of Teacher Education
San Diego State University
San Diego, California

Dr. C. Frederick Risinger
Director, Professional
 Development and Social
 Studies Education
Indiana University
Bloomington, Indiana

Sara Miranda Sanchez
Elementary and Early
 Childhood Curriculum
 Coordinator
Albuquerque Public Schools
Albuquerque, New Mexico

Contributing Authors

Dr. Carol Berkin
Professor of History
Baruch College and the
 Graduate Center
The City University of New York
New York, New York

Lee A. Chase
Staff Development Specialist
Chesterfield County
 Public Schools
Chesterfield County, Virginia

Dr. Jim Cummins
Professor of Curriculum
Ontario Institute for Studies
 in Education
University of Toronto
Toronto, Canada

Dr. Allen D. Glenn
Professor and Dean Emeritus
College of Education
Curriculum and Instruction
University of Washington
Seattle, Washington

Dr. Carole L. Hahn
Professor, Educational Studies
Emory University
Atlanta, Georgia

Dr. M. Gail Hickey
Professor of Education
Indiana University-Purdue
 University
Ft. Wayne, Indiana

Dr. Bonnie Meszaros
Associate Director
Center for Economic Education
 and Entrepreneurship
University of Delaware
Newark, Delaware

ISBN 0-328-03073-2

6 7 8 9 10-V084-11 10 09 08 07 06 05

© Scott Foresman 4 VA

Contents

Unit 4: The Founding of a New Nation

Unit 5: The Civil War and After

Unit 6: The Twentieth Century and Beyond

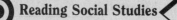
Main Idea and Details

Directions: A main idea is the most important idea in a paragraph or passage. The supporting details give more information about the main idea. Read the paragraph. Answer the questions that follow. Fill in the circle next to the correct answer.

> Virginia is a land with many interesting features. These features include rivers and other waterways. The Chesapeake Bay is one of Virginia's most important waterways. People sell and eat the oysters, crabs, and other fish that come from its waters. People also use the Chesapeake for recreation. At the southern end of the Chesapeake lies the harbor of Hampton Roads—one of the busiest ports in the United States. Here ships carrying goods are loaded and unloaded.

1. Which of the following sentences states the main idea of the paragraph?
   - Ⓐ Hampton Roads is one of the busiest ports in the United States.
   - Ⓑ People use the Chesapeake Bay for recreation.
   - Ⓒ The Chesapeake Bay is one of Virginia's most important waterways.
   - Ⓓ Virginia is a land with many interesting features.

2. Which of the following details does NOT support the main idea of the paragraph?
   - Ⓐ People sell and eat seafood that comes from the Chesapeake Bay.
   - Ⓑ Virginia has a variety of rivers and other waterways, including the Chesapeake Bay.
   - Ⓒ The Chesapeake Bay is a place for swimming and boating.
   - Ⓓ The Chesapeake Bay features one of the busiest ports in the United States.

3. Suppose you were asked to add another supporting detail to the paragraph. Which of the following details would best support the main idea?
   - Ⓐ Water has shaped many of Virginia's natural landmarks.
   - Ⓑ The Chesapeake Bay separates Virginia's Eastern Shore from the mainland.
   - Ⓒ The Potomac, the Rappahanock, the York, and the James flow eastward toward the Chesapeake Bay.
   - Ⓓ The Chesapeake Bay provides jobs for people in the tourism and fishing industries.

4. A paragraph's title should reflect its main idea. Which of the following titles would you choose for the paragraph above?
   - Ⓐ The Waterways of Virginia
   - Ⓑ The Chesapeake Bay: Virginia's Most Vital Waterway
   - Ⓒ The Seafood Industry in Virginia
   - Ⓓ Recreation and Tourism in Virginia

 Notes for Home: Your child learned to identify a main idea and supporting details in a paragraph or passage.
Home Activity: Read an article from a newspaper or magazine with your child. Help your child identify the main idea and supporting details in a paragraph or passage from the article.

© Scott Foresman 4 VA

Vocabulary Preview

Directions: These are the vocabulary words from Chapter 1. Choose the vocabulary from the box that best completes each sentence. Write the word on the line provided.

horizon	natural resource	mineral	climate
hemisphere	renewable resource	fossil fuel	temperate
continent	nonrenewable resource	erosion	drought
peninsula	pollute	conserve	habitat

1. A natural resource that can be replaced or replenished is called a _____.

2. A _____ is something that comes from the earth and is removed by mining.

3. A _____ is formed inside the earth from plants that lived long ago.

4. To _____ is to keep something from becoming damaged or lost.

5. A _____ is a period when rainfall is far below normal.

6. The point where earth and sky appear to meet is the _____.

7. A place is called _____ when it is neither too hot nor too cold.

8. The wearing away of soil by water and wind is_____.

9. A place where an animal lives is a _____.

10. A _____ is a big body of land on the surface of the earth.

11. A place's _____ is the weather it has over a long period.

12. To _____ is to make air, water, or soil dirty.

13. A _____ is a piece of land bordered by water on three sides.

14. A material found in nature that people use is a _____.

15. A natural resource that cannot be replaced is a _____.

16. Each half of the earth is known as a_____.

Notes for Home: Your child learned the vocabulary terms for Chapter 1.
Home Activity: Discuss the term *natural resources* with your child. Share examples of natural resources in your community and the surrounding area.

Lesson 1: Explore Virginia

Directions: Virginia has a variety of unique features. Write the number of each item in column A on the blank next to its example in Column B.

Column A	Column B
1. Northern Neck, Middle Peninsula, The Peninsula	_____ islands that lie along the coast of eastern Virginia
	_____ natural body of water located in the Great Dismal Swamp
2. Chesapeake Bay	_____ pieces of land between the main rivers of eastern Virginia
3. Hampton Roads	
4. Mt. Rogers	_____ A separate region of Virginia connected with the mainland by the Chesapeake Bay Bridge–Tunnel
5. Chincoteague, Assateague	_____ a major waterway that separates one part of Virginia from the mainland
6. Lake Drummond	_____ Virginia's tallest peak, located in the Blue Ridge Mountain range
7. Eastern Shore	
8. Washington D.C.	_____ the Capital of the United States, located on Virgina's border
	_____ a Virginia port that is one of the busiest ports in the United States

Directions: Answer the following questions on the lines provided.

9. How has water shaped Virginia's landscape?

_____

_____

10. Why is the Chesapeake Bay so important to Virginians?

_____

_____

Notes for Home: Your child learned about the interesting features and landforms of Virginia.
Home Activity: Discuss the term "land form" with your child. Ask your child to describe interesting features and landforms of your own community.

© Scott Foresman 4 VA

Wish You Were Here

Postcards have been a popular way to keep in touch with friends and family since the late 1800s. The early 20th century "view cards" on pages 18–19 show the variety of landscapes and landmarks found in Virginia.

Directions: Design a postcard for your region of Virginia. Then present your postcard to the class.

1. In the space below, design a postcard that shows an interesting landscape or landmark in your region.

2. Write the name and location of the landscape or landmark at the top of the postcard.

3. On the lines provided or on a separate sheet of paper, write a brief message to a friend or family member. Tell him or her about the landscape or landmark that's on your postcard.

_____

_____

_____

_____

4. Present your postcard to the class.

Notes for Home: Your child designed a postcard from your region of Virginia and presented it to the class.
Home Activity: With your child, discuss the similarities and differences between the ways people keep in touch today and the ways people kept in touch in the late 1800s.

4 Inside the Smithsonian

Workbook

Name _____ Date _____

Lesson 2: Virginia: Handle with Care

Directions: Complete the chart with information about Virginia's natural resources. Then answer the questions that follow.

Virginia's Natural Resources		
Resource	**Renewable or Nonrenewable?**	**Purpose**
coal		
trees		
soil		

1. How does water runoff harm Virginia's water supply?

   _____

   _____

   _____

2. What are some ways that people can conserve natural resources?

   _____

   _____

3. Why is the Nora Gas Field important to Virginia?

   _____

4. When gold was mined in Virginia, in what part of the state was most of the gold found?

   _____

   _____

Notes for Home: Your child learned about Virginia's natural resources.
Home Activity: Work with your child to list specific ways your family can conserve natural resources in your everyday lives.

© Scott Foresman 4 VA

Name _____ Date _____

Lesson 3: Natural Virginia

Directions: Virginia has a temperate climate and a wide variety of plant and animal life. Answer the following questions about Virginia on the lines provided. You may use your textbook.

1. Why is Virginia's climate helpful to farmers who are trying to grow crops?

_____

_____

_____

2. How is the weather in Virginia's mountains different from the weather in other parts of the state?

_____

_____

_____

3. Why are there so many different kinds of plants in Virginia? Who wrote *Notes on the State of Virginia,* which listed 120 different plants?

_____

_____

_____

4. Where in Virginia is Skyline Drive located? Why is it famous?

_____

_____

_____

5. How do Virginia's plants and landforms affect the state's wildlife population? As more people move to Virginia, what happens to some of the animals that live there?

_____

_____

_____

Notes for Home: Your child learned about Virginia's climate and its plant and animal life.
Home Activity: Review the plants and animals listed and pictured in your child's textbook. Take turns describing specific plants and animals that you have observed in your own surroundings. Help students to understand how weather conditions in your region suit the plant and animal life you have observed.

© Scott Foresman 4 VA

Make Generalizations

Directions: A generalization is a broad statement that applies to a group of people, places, or things. Suppose you are studying climate in Virginia. In this lesson, you have learned that weather in Virginia varies from place to place. You read that temperatures in the mountains are different from temperatures at the coast. Look at the map on page 35. Then make generalizations about the weather in different places in Virginia.

1. How do temperatures at the coast usually differ from temperatures in the mountains?

   _____

   _____

2. Look at the map on page 35. Is one part of the state likely to be cooler than other parts? Write one sentence that summarizes what you have found.

   _____

   _____

3. Which places are probably colder in winter—cities and towns in the Tidewater Region such as Virginia Beach or cities and towns in the Blue Ridge Mountain Region such as Roanoke? Explain your generalization.

   _____

   _____

   _____

4. How does the map on page 35 help to prove your generalizations about Virginia's weather?

   _____

   _____

   _____

5. What probably draws people to the Tidewater Region of Virginia? Make a generalization based on what you know about the location of this region.

   _____

   _____

   _____

Notes for Home: Your child learned to make generalizations based on facts.
Home Activity: With your child, take turns making generalizations about people, places, and things and then supporting them with facts.

Vocabulary Review

Directions: Use the vocabulary words from Chapter 1 to complete the crossword puzzle.

Across

3. a material found in nature that people use

7. what we call a place that is neither too hot nor too cold

9. a place where an animal lives

11. to keep something from becoming damaged or lost

12. a period when rainfall is far below normal

13. a piece of land bordered by water on three sides

16. one half of the earth

Down

1. a natural resource that cannot be replaced

2. a place's weather over a long period

4. a natural resource that can be replaced or replenished

5. a big body of land on the surface of the earth

6. a material formed inside the earth from decayed plants that lived long ago

8. to make something dirty

10. the point where earth and sky appear to meet

14. the wearing away of soil by water and wind

15. something that comes from the earth and is removed by mining

Notes for Home: Your child learned the vocabulary terms for Chapter 1.
Home Activity: Take turns with your child using three or four of the terms in this chapter in complete sentences. See how many sentences you can create using one word.

© Scott Foresman 4 VA

Name _____ Date _____

Vocabulary Preview

Directions: These are the vocabulary words from Chapter 2. How much do you know about these words? Match each vocabulary word to its meaning. Write the number of the word on the blank next to its meaning. You may use your textbook.

1. tide

2. transportation

3. population density

4. plateau

5. textile

6. ridge

7. deep mining

8. surface mining

9. subsistence farming

10. barter

_____ a large, high, almost level piece of land

_____ tunneling into the earth and removing coal

_____ the number of people living in a particular area

_____ trade without using money

_____ stripping off the earth and rock that lies above the coal

_____ the daily rising and falling of oceans and the waters connected to them

_____ raising your own food and making the things you need

_____ a woven fabric

_____ the moving of people or goods

_____ a line of mountains and hills

 Notes for Home: Your child learned the vocabulary terms for Chapter 2.
Home Activity: Practice saying, spelling, or using these words correctly with your child.

Lesson 1: Virginia's Tidewater

Directions: The Atlantic Ocean, the Chesapeake Bay, and many rivers shape Virginia's important Tidewater Region. Answer the following questions about the Tidewater Region on the lines provided. You may use your textbook.

1. Why is the eastern part of Virginia known as the Tidewater Region? Name three communities in the Tidewater Region.

   _____

   _____

   _____

2. How were the rivers of the Tidewater helpful to people living four hundred years ago?

   _____

   _____

   _____

3. What is the Coastal Plain?

   _____

   _____

   _____

4. Why has the Tidewater always been a good area for farming?

   _____

   _____

   _____

5. What businesses and industries have been built in the Tidewater?

   _____

   _____

   _____

   _____

Notes for Home: Your child learned about Virginia's Tidewater Region.
Home Activity: Spend time discussing with your child how the Tidewater Region benefits Virginia. Mention the various waterways; important crops such as peanuts, cotton, and soybeans; seafood; and ships.

© Scott Foresman 4 VA

Name _____ Date _____

Lesson 2: The Piedmont of Virginia

Directions: Virginia's Piedmont Region is the site of several important cities. Using information from this lesson, circle the term in parentheses that best completes each sentence.

1. The Piedmont Region is named for its location near the

   (Chesapeake Bay, Blue Ridge Mountains).

2. The (fall line, plateau) is the place where waterfalls separate the Piedmont from

   the Tidewater.

3. Ships carrying goods could not travel past the falls, so the area became

   (a busy marketplace, an open field).

4. Factories built at the falls used (rushing water, fertile soil) to power machines.

5. The city of (Petersburg, Fredericksburg) grew at the falls of the Appomattox River.

6. The city of Danville, on the Dan River, became a center for manufacturing (textiles, ships).

7. Northern Piedmont has a (low, high) population density.

8. The city of (Alexandria, Richmond), which is located just south of Washington, D.C.,

   grew up as a trading center on the Potomac River.

9. Today, a (highway, mass transit system) known as the Metro links many communities in

   Virginia to our nation's capital.

10. The city of (Alexandria, Charlottesville) is home to the University of Virginia,

    which opened in 1825.

© Scott Foresman 4 VA

Notes for Home: Your child learned about Virginia's Piedmont Region.
Home Activity: Show your child a map of Virginia and point out the Piedmont Region. Ask your child to locate some of the cities discussed in the lesson. Talk about some of the most interesting features of these cities.

Name _____ Date _____

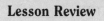

Lesson 3: Virginia's Blue Ridge

Directions: Virginia's Blue Ridge Mountains, once a barrier to settlers, draw tourists from all over the country. Explain each term below and tell how it relates to the Blue Ridge Mountain area. Write your answers on the lines provided. You may use your textbook.

1. ridge

_____

_____

_____

2. Appalachian Mountain system

_____

_____

_____

3. natural barrier

_____

_____

_____

4. Roanoke Gap and Harpers Ferry

_____

_____

_____

5. Shenandoah National Park

_____

_____

_____

Notes for Home: Your child learned about Virginia's Blue Ridge Mountain Region.
Home Activity: Has your family ever been to the mountains or to a national park? Discuss with your child any mountains or national parks you have visited or would like to visit.

© Scott Foresman 4 VA

Workbook

Lesson 4: The Valley and Ridge Region

Directions: The Valley and Ridge Region features beautiful valleys and many natural wonders. Write the number of each item in Column A on the blank next to its example in Column B.

Column A	Column B

Column A

1. Allegheny Mountains

2. Valley of Virginia

3. Shenandoah Valley

4. Massanutten Mountain

5. Natural Chimneys, Tunnel, and Bridge

6. Luray Caverns

7. Cumberland Gap

8. Wilderness Road

Column B

_____ a narrow gap found at the far western tip of Virginia that served as an important passageway to the west

_____ the northernmost part of the Valley of Virginia

_____ a 50-mile-long ridge that splits the Shenandoah Valley down the middle

_____ the western part of the Valley and Ridge Region along the West Virginia border

_____ caves, or underground spaces, formed from the action of water on rock

_____ a road through the Cumberland Gap that led settlers from Virginia to Kentucky and beyond

_____ the eastern part of the Valley and Ridge Region

_____ rock forms created by water wearing away rock over a long period of time

Directions: Answer the following questions on the lines provided.

9. Why are the cities of Roanoke and Bristol important to the Valley and Ridge Region?

_____

_____

10. What did Daniel Boone accomplish in the Valley and Ridge Region?

_____

_____

Notes for Home: Your child learned about Virginia's Valley and Ridge Region.
Home Activity: Discuss with your child any natural wonders that your family has observed firsthand. Talk about why these features of nature are so fascinating to people.

Name _____ Date _____

Lesson 5: The Appalachian Plateau

Directions: The Appalachian Plateau in Virginia is a small, rugged region known for coal mining. Suppose that you are going to write an article about the Appalachian Plateau. Complete the chart below to help you get started. You may use your textbook.

The Appalachian Plateau

WHERE is it located and WHAT is its largest city?	
WHAT does it look like and HOW was it formed?	
WHY is this region important?	
HOW is the land affected by mining?	
WHY have no large urban areas developed here?	

Notes for Home: Your child learned about Virginia's Appalachian Plateau.
Home Activity: Find out what your child has heard about coal and mining. Talk about the uses for coal and the challenges of working as a miner.

© Scott Foresman 4 VA

Name _____ Date _____

Read an Elevation Map

Directions: An elevation map shows the elevation of a given area. Read the elevation map and answer the questions that follow.

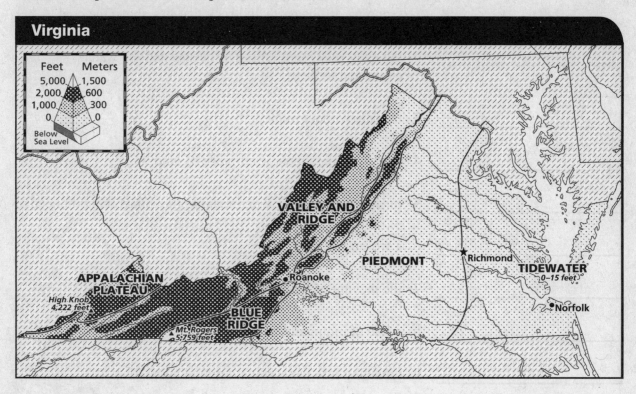

1. Which three regions have the highest elevations?

   _____

2. Which two have the lowest elevations?

   _____

3. What is the highest elevation in the Appalachian Plateau?

   _____

4. At what elevations are the state's highest and lowest points?

   _____

   _____

Notes for Home: Your child learned how to read an elevation map.
Home Activity: Work with your child to locate your own community on an elevation map.

Vocabulary Review

Directions: Write each vocabulary word from Chapter 2 beside its example or description.

_____ **1.** stripping off the earth and rock that lies above the coal

_____ **2.** the daily rising and falling of oceans and the waters connected to them

_____ **3.** to trade without money

_____ **4.** a large, high, almost level piece of land

_____ **5.** raising your own food and making the things that you need

_____ **6.** a woven fabric

_____ **7.** the moving of people or goods

_____ **8.** a line of mountains and hills

_____ **9.** tunneling into the earth and removing coal

_____ **10.** the number of people living in a particular area

Directions: Write a postcard to someone from another state. Use at least four vocabulary words.

© Scott Foresman 4 VA

Notes for Home: Your child learned the vocabulary terms for Chapter 2.
Home Activity: Read aloud the letter your child wrote about the state of Virginia. Discuss the vocabulary terms and how they illustrate what is interesting about your state.

Name _____   Date _____

^{UNIT}
1 Project   Eye on Our Region

Use with Page 72.

Directions: Take visitors on a video tour that shows what's great about your region of Virginia. In a group, choose an interesting topic about your region. Then present your video tour to the class.

1. The topic we chose about our region of Virginia is _____.

2. Here are some places and landmarks in our region that we will include in our map:

   _____.

3. Below are some facts that we gathered about our topic. The ✔ shows which fact I will illustrate for our video tour:

   _____ **A.** _____

   _____ **B.** _____

   _____ **C.** _____

   _____ **D.** _____

4. For our video tour, we will arrange our illustrations in this order:

   _____

   _____

✔ **Checklist for Students**

_____ We chose a topic about our region of Virginia.

_____ We made a map of our region.

_____ We found information and made a list of facts about our topic.

_____ We drew pictures that illustrated our facts and described each picture in a sentence or two.

_____ We shared what we learned in a video tour by putting our pictures together and describing them to the class.

 Notes for Home: Your child learned to describe an interesting topic about our region with illustrations.
Home Activity: Have your child describe the video tour presented in class today and discuss some other interesting topics about our region with your child.

Name _____ Date _____

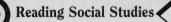
Cause and Effect

Directions: A cause is why something happens. An effect is what happens as a result of a cause. Circle the letter of the effect that goes best with each numbered cause. Use information on page 79 of your textbook.

1. In the 1400s, there was a demand for Asian goods.

   Ⓐ Travel to Asia was long and expensive.

   Ⓑ Europeans set out to find a quick, easy route to Asia.

   Ⓒ Christopher Columbus was an explorer.

   Ⓓ People did not understand the world as we do today.

2. Columbus thought he could find a fast route by sailing west across the Atlantic Ocean.

   Ⓐ Travel in the 1400s was difficult.

   Ⓑ The Bahamas are located between North and South America.

   Ⓒ Columbus named the island San Salvador.

   Ⓓ Columbus set sail in 1492 and reached an island in the Bahamas.

3. Some people in the Americas had vast treasures of gold, silver, and jewels.

   Ⓐ Columbus did not find a shortcut to Asia.

   Ⓑ People learned that the colonies of North and South America existed.

   Ⓒ Spain sent armies across the ocean.

   Ⓓ Columbus found a rich and wonderful land.

4. Spain conquered the native people and took their treasures.

   Ⓐ Spain sent armies across the ocean.

   Ⓑ Columbus's discovery was important.

   Ⓒ Gold, silver, and jewels were valuable to Spain.

   Ⓓ Spain became rich and powerful.

5. The English admired Spain's success.

   Ⓐ England sent explorers and settlers to North America too.

   Ⓑ England is north of Spain.

   Ⓒ England had explorers, too.

   Ⓓ There were no easy shortcuts to Asia.

© Scott Foresman 4 VA

 Notes for Home: Your child learned to identify causes and effects in a paragraph or passage.
Home Activity: Read an article from a newspaper with your child. Help your child identify the causes and effects in a paragraph or passage from the article.

Lesson 2: The Powhatan Way of Life

Directions: The Powhatan way of life was rich in culture and well adapted to the Tidewater's available resources. Suppose you are going to write an article about the Powhatan way of life. Complete the chart below to help you get started. You may use your textbook.

The Powhatan Way of Life	
WHY did the Powhatan build villages near rivers in the Tidewater Region?	
HOW were Powhatan houses built?	
WHAT foods did the Powhatan grow, forage, and hunt?	
WHO ruled the Powhatan groups?	
WHY were the Powhatan a weakened people by the early 1600s?	

Notes for Home: Your child learned about the Powhatan way of life in the Tidewater Region of Virginia. **Home Activity:** Review the pictures of Powhatans and Powhatan villages in your child's textbook. Take turns describing materials in nature that the Powhatan used for shelter, clothes, and food. Help your child to understand how the Powhatan way of life was deeply connected to nature.

Name _____ Date _____

Use with Pages 94–95.

American Indian Artifacts

By the time the Europeans began exploring the Americas, North America had been home to many different groups of American Indians for thousands of years.

Directions: Complete the chart with information about the artifacts shown on pages 94–95. These artifacts represent some of the work of American Indians from areas throughout North America.

Artifact	What Was Its Purpose?
Alibamu Ornaments	
Pawnee War Bonnet	
Beaded Pouch	
Comanche Parfleche Case	
Lakota Cradleboard	

Notes for Home: Your child learned about American Indians from areas throughout North America.
Home Activity: Ask your child about the American Indian artifacts studied in class. With your child, compare the American Indian artifacts with items having similar purposes that your family may own.

Lesson 3: Winds of Change

Directions: American Indians in Virginia began having contact with Europeans in the 1500s. Answer the following questions on the lines provided. You may use your textbook.

1. What happened in the year 1492?

_____
_____
_____

2. Why did Europeans begin to explore the Americas?

_____
_____
_____

3. Who was Giovanni da Verrazano?

_____
_____
_____

4. Why did Don Luis leave his Tidewater village in the 1500s? Why did he return ten years later?

_____
_____
_____

5. Why did American Indians in Virginia always fear the return of the Spanish explorers?

_____
_____
_____

Notes for Home: Your child learned about the first contacts between American Indians in Virginia and Europeans in the 1500s.
Home Activity: Review what happened between American Indians in Virginia and Europeans. Have your child describe how the relationship between American Indians and Europeans changed.

Use with Pages 100–101.

Identify Fact, Opinion, and Point of View

Directions: A fact is something that can be proven to be true. An opinion is a person's belief or judgment. Point of view describes something as one person or group would see it. Read the following sentences. Identify each as either a fact or an opinion. Write *F* for "fact" or *O* for "opinion" on each blank line provided.

_____ 1. The Powhatan belonged to the Algonquian group of American Indians.

_____ 2. Chief Powhatan's daughter Pocahontas married an Englishman.

_____ 3. Chief Powhatan was wise to distrust the Europeans.

_____ 4. The Powhatan made tools from stone, shells, animal bones, and wood.

_____ 5. European methods of farming were better than the Powhatan's farming practices.

_____ 6. Chief Powhatan was a great leader of his people.

_____ 7. Rivers provided many natural resources for the Powhatan.

Directions: Identify the point of view from which each of the following sentences is written. Write *Spanish* or *Powhatan* on the lines provided.

_____ 8. Spanish exploration of the Americas brought great benefits to the Powhatan.

_____ 9. The Powhatan were bound to fail in their struggle against the Spanish explorers.

_____ 10. The Spanish did not respect the Powhatan way of life.

Notes for Home: Your child learned how to distinguish fact from opinion and how to identify point of view.
Home Activity: With your child, read a brief newspaper article about a current event in the news. Take turns identifying facts and opinions in the article. Then discuss the point or points of view that are described in the article.

Vocabulary Review

Directions: Use each of the vocabulary terms from Chapter 3 in a sentence. Write the sentences on the lines provided. You may use your glossary.

1. nomad

_____

_____

2. agriculture

_____

_____

3. government

_____

_____

4. epidemic

_____

_____

5. forage

_____

_____

6. mission

_____

_____

7. interpreter

_____

_____

Notes for Home: Your child learned the vocabulary terms for Chapter 3.
Home Activity: Discuss the vocabulary terms and how they relate to American Indians and European explorers in Virginia.

Vocabulary Preview

Directions: These are the vocabulary words from Chapter 4. How much do you know about these words? Match each vocabulary word to its meaning. Write the number of the word on the blank next to its meaning. You may use your textbook.

1. share ———— a group that makes rules and decisions

2. charter ———— a land that is settled far from the country that governs it

3. council ———— part ownership of a company

4. colony ———— a written list of rights granted by a ruler or government

Directions: Choose the vocabulary word from above that best completes each sentence. Write the word on the line provided.

5. In 1583, people from England traveled across the ocean to establish a

_____ in North America.

6. She owns a _____ of the company and will get some of the money

the company makes.

7. The _____ gave British settlers permission to claim lands in

North America.

8. A _____ of settlers ran day-to-day affairs in Virginia.

© Scott Foresman 4 VA

Notes for Home: Your child learned the vocabulary terms for Chapter 4.
Home Activity: Practice saying, spelling, and using these words correctly with your child.

Lesson 1: The English in Virginia

Directions: In 1578, people from England tried to cross the Atlantic and reach the Americas. Using information from this lesson, complete the outline with information from this lesson. You may use your textbook.

The First English Colonies in North America

I. The First Attempt: Sir Humphrey Gilbert

    A. 1578: _____ gave Sir Humphrey Gilbert a

    _____ to start a colony in North America.

    B. Gilbert landed in present-day _____; he drowned during a storm before he could explore more of North America.

II. Roanoke Island and Virginia

    A. 1584: Sir Humphrey Gilbert's half brother, _____, sent two ships to explore the coast of North America.

        1. The ships were commanded by _____ and Philip Amadas.

        2. They reached _____, off the coast of present-day North Carolina.

    C. 1585: _____ led the first expedition of settlers to Virginia.

        1. Relations between the _____ and the English settlers turned hostile.

        2. The settlers ran out of food; Sir Francis Drake took settlers back to England.

III. The Lost Colony

    A. 1587: _____ led colonists to settle along

    _____. The settlers ended up on Roanoke Island. They faced hunger and disease.

    B. He returned to England for more supplies but could not return for three years. He found the settlement deserted.

Notes for Home: Your child learned about England's first attempts to establish colonies in North America.
Home Activity: Spend time discussing with your child the places where the English first claimed land in North America. Identify these places on a map of the United States.

© Scott Foresman 4 VA

Lesson 2: Jamestown

Directions: In 1607, the English finally succeeded in setting up a colony in Virginia. Sequence the events listed below in the order in which they took place by numbering them from 1 to 10. You may use your textbook.

_____ 1. The three ships from England landed at Cape Henry in Virginia.

_____ 2. The English decided on a settlement and named it James Fort, or Jamestown.

_____ 3. England's new king, James I, granted a charter to the Virginia Company to start a new Virginia colony.

_____ 4. Few colonists listened to Captain John Smith's warnings about the possibility of a Powhatan attack.

_____ 5. Captain Christopher Newport commanded on expedition that set sail from England, carrying colonists to Virginia.

_____ 6. Colonists sailed up the James River and met a number of Powhatan groups.

_____ 7. A group of wealthy people formed the Virginia Company of London, or just the Virginia Company.

_____ 8. The colonists learned to appreciate John Smith.

_____ 9. The king's council in London named a council of Virginia settlers to run the new colony.

_____ 10. The settlers built shelters, planted crops, and built a log fort.

Notes for Home: Your child learned about the founding of England's Jamestown colony in Virginia.
Home Activity: Review with your child the features of the site chosen for the Jamestown settlement and the reasons why the site might cause problems for the colonists.

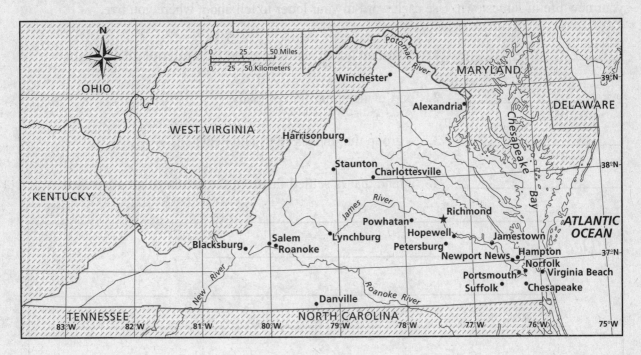
Understand Latitude and Longitude

Directions: Mapmakers draw latitude and longitude lines on maps or globes to give an "address" for cities, towns, and other places on Earth. Use the map to answer questions 1–4.

1. Which city shown on the map is closest to 39°N and 77°W?

   _____

2. Which cities along the James River are located between 37°N and 38°N latitude and 77°W and 78°W longitude?

   _____

3. Between which two degrees of latitude does the southern border of Virginia rest?

   _____

4. Which lines of latitude and longitude are closest to Jamestown?

   _____

Notes for Home: Your child learned how to use latitude and longitude on a map.
Home Activity: Take turns with your child identifying the latitude and longitude locations of other towns and cities in Virginia.

Vocabulary Review

Directions: Write each vocabulary word from Chapter 4 beside its description. Then pretend you are Captain John Smith. Write a letter to someone back in England about your new life in Jamestown. Use each word in your letter to tell about where you live.

_____   **1.**   a written list of rights granted by a ruler or government

_____   **2.**   part ownership of a company

_____   **3.**   a group that makes rules and decisions

_____   **4.**   a land that is settled far from the country that governs it

Dear _____ *,*

_____

_____

_____

_____

_____

_____

_____

_____

_____

Best Wishes,
John Smith

© Scott Foresman 4 VA

Notes for Home: Your child learned the vocabulary terms for Chapter 4.
Home Activity: Read aloud the letter your child wrote about colony life in Jamestown from the point of view of Captain John Smith. Discuss the vocabulary terms and how they relate to the organization of England's first colony in Virginia.

Vocabulary Preview

Directions: These are the vocabulary words from Chapter 5. How much do you know about these words? Choose the vocabulary word from the box that best completes each sentence. Write the word on the line provided. You may use your textbook.

malaria	indentured servant	veto
cash crop	enslaved	plantation
export	assembly	self-government
money		

1. A group that meets to make laws is called an _____.

2. To send goods to another country for sale is to _____.

3. A _____ is something that is grown to sell rather than to use.

4. _____ means making and enforcing laws for oneself.

5. People with the deadly disease called _____ get chills and fever

   and sometimes die.

6. An _____ was someone who agreed to work without pay for a

   certain time.

7. People taken from their homes against their will and said to be owned by someone

   else were _____.

8. A farming settlement was called a _____.

9. To _____ means to stop an act from going into effect.

10. Coins or bills used for trading goods are known as _____.

Notes for Home: Your child learned the vocabulary terms for Chapter 5.
Home Activity: Discuss the term *self-government* with your child and compare it to a representative system of government.

Lesson 1: A Struggle for Survival

Directions: Use the terms in the box to complete each sentence with information from Lesson 1. You may use your textbook.

Pocahontas	Lord De La Warr
Mistress Forrest	Chickahominy River
Anne Burras	Jamestown
Sir Thomas Gates	Fort Henrico

1. Colonists in _____ struggled to survive the winter.

2. _____ was shocked by the conditions in the colony and told the starving people to return to England with him.

3. In 1611, the colonists built _____ on the James River.

4. Captain Smith explored the _____ and was captured by a Powhatan hunting party.

5. The first two English women to live in Jamestown were _____

   and _____ .

6. Chief Powhatan's daughter was named _____ .

7. The Virginia Company gave _____ more power to govern the colonists.

Directions: Answer the following questions on the lines provided.

8. What problems did the colonists struggle with?

   _____

9. What factors helped the Jamestown colony survive?

   _____

10. Why was John Smith an important leader for the colonists?

   _____

   _____

 Notes for Home: Your child learned about the colonists' struggle to survive in Jamestown.
Home Activity: Has your family ever grown vegetables in a garden? Discuss with your child how difficult it is to grow your own food and how difficult it would be to survive on only the food from the garden.

© Scott Foresman 4 VA

Lesson 2: The Colony Gains a Foothold

Directions: Explain each term below and tell how it relates to the changes and growth in the Virginia colony. You may use your textbook.

1. John Rolfe

   _____

   _____

   _____

2. cash crop

   _____

   _____

   _____

3. export

   _____

   _____

   _____

4. House of Burgesses

   _____

   _____

   _____

5. General Assembly

   _____

   _____

   _____

_____

Notes for Home: Your child learned about the changes and growth that took place in Jamestown in the 1610s.
Home Activity: With your child, identify some cash crops that are important to your region. Discuss how the crop affects your local economy.

Lesson 3: Conflict with the Powhatan

Directions: Many misunderstandings between the English and the Powhatan led to violence. Complete the graphic organizer below with details from your textbook.

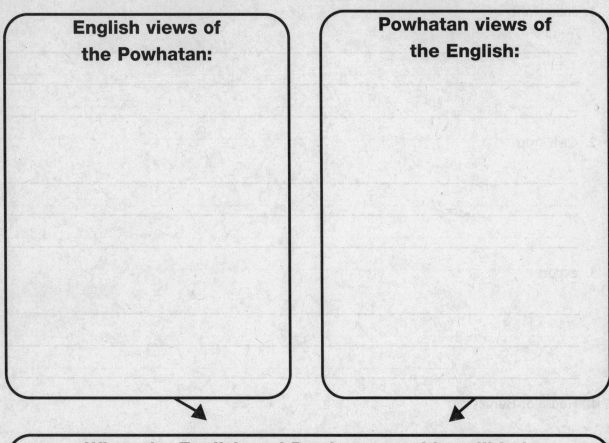

English views of the Powhatan:

Powhatan views of the English:

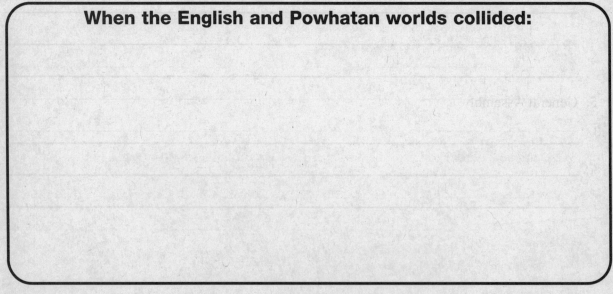

When the English and Powhatan worlds collided:

Notes for Home: Your child learned about the causes and effects of misunderstandings between the English and the Powhatan.

Home Activity: Discuss with your child some of the reasons why people disagree with one another. Talk about how people can work together to solve their conflicts or misunderstandings.

© Scott Foresman 4 VA

Lesson 4: Changes in the Colony

Directions: The Virginia colony continued to grow larger and stronger. Answer the following questions on the lines provided. You may use your textbook.

1. What problems did the new colony still face in 1622? What did King James do in 1624 to deal with the problems?

   _____

   _____

   _____

2. Why did the colonists dislike it when people from England told them what to do?

   _____

   _____

3. Virginia grew larger and stronger. Why, then, were many Virginia settlers unhappy?

   _____

   _____

   _____

4. Why did Opechancanough lead another attack on the English colonists?

   _____

   _____

5. What happened after the war between the Powhatan and the English ended?

   _____

   _____

Notes for Home: Your child learned about the changes that took place in the Virginia colony.
Home Activity: Discuss with your child the concept of self-government.

Use Map Scale and Inset Maps

Directions: A map scale shows the relationship between the size of the real area and the size of the map. A map's scale shows the real distance between places. An inset map shows one area on a map at a larger scale. Read the map and answer the questions that follow.

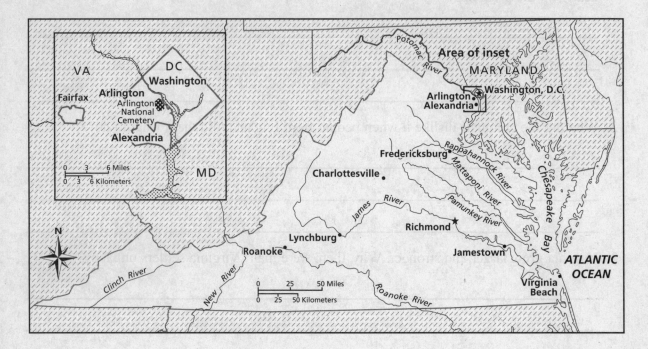

1. About how far is Alexandria from Jamestown?

_____

2. You want to know where Arlington National Cemetery is located. Which map would you use?

_____

3. Near what national capital is Arlington National Cemetery located?

_____

4. You want to find out the distance between Jamestown and Washington, D.C. Which map would you use?

_____

Notes for Home: Your child learned how to use map scale and an inset map.
Home Activity: Find a map of your state that includes an inset map of a city or area within the state. Work with your child to locate your own community or city on the map and to figure out distances and locations from that point.

© Scott Foresman 4 VA

Vocabulary Review

Directions: Find and circle the vocabulary words from Chapter 5 in the word search puzzle below. On a separate sheet of paper, use five of the words to write five complete sentences. You may use your textbook.

malaria	indentured servant	veto
cash crop	enslaved	plantation
export	assembly	self-government
money		

```
R  N  S  I  H  L  C  A  S  H  C  R  O  P  L  O  A
H  M  Y  -  T  A  S  S  E  M  B  L  Y  L  B  J  Q
S  O  Z  D  G  U  R  F  H  L  K  V  V  A  R  G  N
Z  N  C  E  N  S  L  A  V  E  D  D  D  N  W  F  M
J  E  E  N  Q  R  H  T  J  X  E  B  Y  T  C  D  A
V  Y  K  T  K  U  W  S  I  P  K  -  P  A  V  K  L
C  Q  T  Q  L  W  V  X  R  O  O  A  E  T  A  C  A
D  N  U  -  U  Y  E  M  O  R  J  T  A  I  W  B  R
Q  L  C  M  E  I  T  B  W  T  F  W  O  O  T  Q  I
X  R  W  L  I  D  O  P  I  E  U  P  P  N  U  R  A
R  J  K  N  R  K  Y  Y  P  U  G  Y  Q  K  P  V  S
U  G  S  E  L  F  -  G  O  V  E  R  N  M  E  N  T
B  W  H  P  S  E  I  K  U  S  P  C  H  T  L  T  L
I  N  D  E  N  T  U  R  E  D  S  E  R  V  A  N  T
K  U  P  A  O  J  H  R  A  O  S  E  B  W  M  X  D
```

Notes for Home: Your child learned the vocabulary terms for Chapter 5.
Home Activity: Review the vocabulary terms with your child. Work together to see how many sentences you can create using one vocabulary term.

UNIT 2 Project On the Spot

Directions: In a group, make a documentary about the experiences of American Indians or early European settlers. Present your documentary to the class.

1. We will include these topics in our documentary:

   A. What types of homes they lived in:

   _____

   B. What they ate and where they got their food:

   _____

   C. What methods of transportation they used:

   _____

   D. What their environment and surroundings were like:

   _____

   E. What daily life was like for them:

   _____

2. This is what we will include in our diorama:

   _____

   _____

✔ **Checklist for Students**

_____ We found information about Virginia's early settlers.

_____ We wrote sentences about the settlers' experiences.

_____ We made a diorama to show the environment of the settlers.

_____ We presented our diorama to the class and talked about the experiences of Virginia's early inhabitants.

© Scott Foresman 4 VA

Notes for Home: Your child learned about the experiences of early inhabitants of Virginia.
Home Activity: Discuss with your child the similarities and differences between life in Virginia today and life at the time of Virginia's early inhabitants.

Sequence

Directions: Sequence means the order in which things happen. Dates and words such as *meanwhile, during, first, then, next,* and *finally* help signal the sequence of events. Other clues that might be used are dates, times of day, and times of the year. Use page 165 of your textbook to answer the following questions. Fill in the circle next to the correct answer.

1. Which of the following events happened first?
   Ⓐ The Treaty of 1646 was signed.
   Ⓑ 200 settlers formed a volunteer army under Nathaniel Bacon.
   Ⓒ The Powhatan attacked the colonists in 1644.
   Ⓓ The settlers made war on the royal governor.

2. What happened when the governor refused to push the American Indians even farther away?
   Ⓐ The Powhatan attacked the colonists in 1644.
   Ⓑ Settlers moved north of the York River.
   Ⓒ The colonists created the Treaty of 1646.
   Ⓓ Colonists formed a volunteer army and made war on the American Indians and the governor.

3. Which of the following lists the sequence of events correctly?
   Ⓐ The Powhatan attack, Treaty of 1646, Bacon's Rebellion
   Ⓑ Treaty of 1646, the Powhatan attack, Bacon's Rebellion
   Ⓒ Bacon's Rebellion, Treaty of 1646, the Powhatan attack
   Ⓓ Treaty of 1646, Bacon's Rebellion, the Powhatan attack

4. What led to conflict between settlers and American Indians in 1660?
   Ⓐ The Powhatan attacked settlers.
   Ⓑ Many indentured servants moved into American Indian territory to start their own farms.
   Ⓒ Leaders drew up the Treaty of 1646, which was unfair to American Indians.
   Ⓓ Nathaniel Bacon led a rebellion.

5. At what point was it clear that the colonists were willing to fight their government?
   Ⓐ immediately following the Powhatan attack
   Ⓑ when the Treaty of 1646 was established
   Ⓒ as many indentured servants began to start their own farms
   Ⓓ when Bacon's Rebellion took place

© Scott Foresman 4 VA

Notes for Home: Your child learned to identify the sequence of events in a paragraph or passage.
Home Activity: Read a newspaper article with your child that discusses a recent event in local, national, or world news. Help your child identify the sequence of events in a paragraph or passage from the article.

Vocabulary Preview

Directions: These are the vocabulary words from Chapter 6. How much do you know about these words? Use these words to complete the crossword puzzle. You may use your textbook.

savings	debt	rebellion
credit	frontier	profit

Across

3. an agreement in which a buyer promises to pay for an item at a later time

4. money set aside to be spent later

6. armed resistance against one's government

Down

1. condition of owing to others more than you have

2. the far edge of a settlement

5. the money made by a business after all its expenses have been paid

© Scott Foresman 4 VA

Lesson 1: Growing Pains in the Colony

Directions: Draw a line from each item in column A to its example in column B.

Column A

1. Cavalier

2. Nathaniel Bacon

3. Old Dominion

4. Sir William Berkeley

5. Jamestown

Column B

a. Charles II's affectionate name for Virginia colony

b. governor of Virginia colony

c. a town burned during Bacon's Rebellion

d. a supporter of King Charles I

e. leader of a rebellion against Virginia's governor

Directions: Answer the following questions on the lines provided.

6. Why did Charles II feel fondness for Virginia?

_____

_____

7. What unpopular rule of Charles II did the governor tell Virginians to follow?

_____

8. Why were many of Virginia's tobacco farmers in debt?

_____

_____

_____

9. Why were Virginians along the frontier unhappy with their governor?

_____

_____

10. What happened in Bacon's Rebellion?

_____

_____

Notes for Home: Your child learned about Bacon's Rebellion and other difficulties in colonial Virginia.
Home Activity: Discuss with your child how a rebellion looks different, depending on your point of view. Ask your child what Governor Berkeley may have thought of the actions of Bacon's followers and what Nathaniel Bacon may have thought of the actions of his followers.

Name _____ Date _____

Lesson 2: New Virginians

Directions: The map below, shows the trade pattern known as the triangular trade.
Write the words *Middle Passage* along the part of the triangle known by this name.
On the lines below the map, explain triangular trade and the Middle Passage.

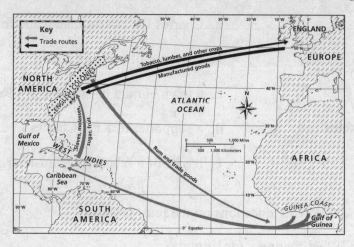

_____

_____

_____

_____

_____

Directions: Answer the following questions on the lines provided.

1. What was the difference between an indentured servant and an enslaved person?

_____

_____

_____

2. Why did lower tobacco prices help slavery increase in Virginia?

_____

_____

_____

 Notes for Home: Your child learned about the arrival of indentured servants and slaves in Virginia.
Home Activity: Analyze with your child the reasons why planters came to depend on the system of slavery. Have your child imagine what he or she would say to a plantation owner about the use of enslaved workers.

© Scott Foresman 4 VA

Take Notes

Directions: Taking notes helps you to understand and remember what you read.
When you take notes, write down the most important thing you read about the topic
and important supporting details. Read the paragraph below. Write the main idea
and supporting details in the spaces provided.

> While Matthew Ashby gained his freedom at the age of 31, he was not
> really free. Because he was a black person, he had limited rights. He
> could not travel without a pass. He could not have weapons. In addition,
> it was illegal for free black people to visit with enslaved people.

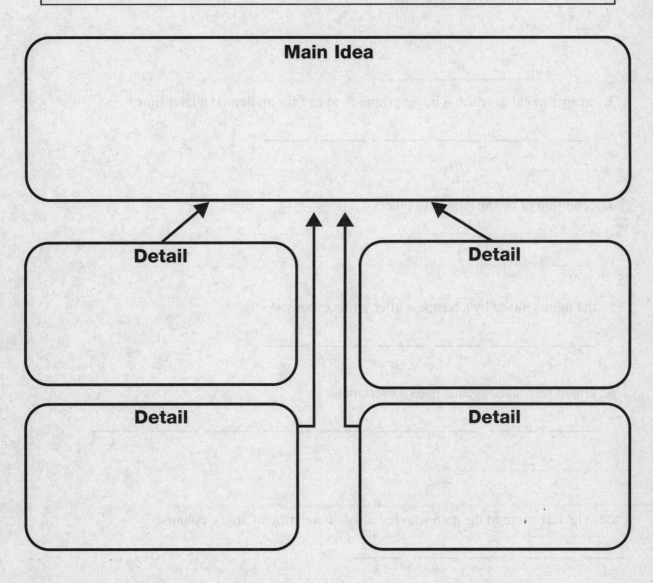

Main Idea

Detail

Detail

Detail

Detail

Vocabulary Review

Directions: Use the vocabulary words from Chapter 6 to complete each item.
Use the numbered letters to answer the clue that follows.

1. the far edge of a settlement

   ___ ___ ___ ___ ___ ___ ___ ___ ___
                 4

2. money set aside to be spent later

   ___ ___ ___ ___ ___ ___ ___ ___ ___
         2

3. an agreement in which a buyer promises to pay for an item at a later time

   ___ ___ ___ ___ ___ ___ ___
   3

4. condition of owing money to others

   ___ ___ ___ ___ ___
           1

5. the money made by a business after all its expenses

   ___ ___ ___ ___ ___ ___

6. armed resistance against one's government

   ___ ___ ___ ___ ___ ___ ___ ___ ___ ___
                                       5

Clue: The last name of the man who led a volunteer army of angry colonists.

___ ___ ___ ___ ___
 1   2   3   4   5

Notes for Home: Your child learned the vocabulary for Chapter 6.
Home Activity: Ask your child to explain how each of the vocabulary words relates to what he or she learned in Chapter 6.

Vocabulary Preview

Directions: Choose the vocabulary word from the box that best completes each sentence. Write the word on the line provided.

capital	ally	boycott
immigrant	tax	congress
treaty	Parliament	militia

1. A(n) _____ is a person or group that helps another reach

   a common goal.

2. A(n) _____ is money a government collects from its people.

3. An army made up of ordinary citizens who can be called together in times of emergency

   is called a(n) _____ .

4. A(n) _____ is a city that serves as the home of a government.

5. One way people protest nonviolently is to _____ , or refuse to buy,

   the goods of the group they are protesting.

6. Britain's lawmaking body is known as _____ .

7. A(n) _____ is someone who moves to one country from another.

8. A(n) _____ is a formal meeting.

9. A(n) _____ is a formal agreement between two nations.

Notes for Home: Your child learned the vocabulary words for Chapter 7.
Home Activity: Practice pronouncing and spelling the vocabulary words with your child. Make sure your child can form and spell the plural form of the words in the list *(capitals, immigrants, treaties, allies, taxes, Parliaments, boycotts* [as noun]*, congresses,* and *militias).*

Name _____ Date _____

Lesson 1: Virginia Grows Up

Directions: Using information from this lesson, circle the term in parentheses that best completes each sentence.

1. After a fire destroyed the main government building, Virginians decided to move their capital from (Middle Plantation, Jamestown) to (Middle Plantation, the Piedmont).

2. Virginians named their new capital (Williamsburg, Shenandoah).

3. In Middle Plantation, the colonists built their first (major government building, college) and named it in honor of (King William and Queen Mary, Sir William Berkeley).

4. In 1716, Alexander Spotswood led explorers over the Blue Ridge Mountains to the (Shenandoah Valley, Tidewater).

5. Spotswood hoped that Virginian settlers would move farther west to keep out the (American Indians, French).

6. Immigrants from (Europe, Asia) settled in the Shenandoah Valley.

7. These immigrants brought (their own ways of living, enslaved people) to Virginia.

8. Soon, settlers moved onto the Piedmont; these settlers included wealthy planters as well as (factory owners, less wealthy planters).

9. In 1750, Dr. Thomas Walker went through the (Cumberland Gap, Shenandoah Valley).

10. Land west of the frontier was home to (Spanish settlers, American Indians).

© Scott Foresman 4 VA

 Notes for Home: Your child learned about how different ways of life developed in colonial Virginia.
Home Activity: Discuss with your child how the various groups in Virginia might have lived. Ask your child to imagine what life was like for a wealthy planter in the Tidewater Region, a poor German farmer on the frontier, and an enslaved African on the Piedmont.

Lesson 2: Trouble on the Frontier

Directions: Write the number of each item in Column A on the blank next to its example in Column B.

Column A

1. George Washington

2. Fort Duquesne

3. Fort Necessity

4. Robert Dinwiddie

5. Chief Cornstalk

Column B

_____ Virginia governor who warned the French that they were building on Virginia's land

_____ French fort captured by Virginians near the end of the French and Indian war

_____ Shawnee leader defeated in Lord Dunmore's War

_____ military leader whose attack on the French marked the start of the French and Indian War

_____ fort that Virginians built

Directions: Answer the following questions on the lines provided.

6. What land did the Virginians, British, French, and American Indians fight over during the French and Indian War?

_____

7. Why did most American Indian groups side with the French?

_____

8. What two valuable lessons did the colonists learn from the French and Indian War?

_____

_____

9. What was the Proclamation of 1763?

_____

_____

10. What caused Lord Dunmore's War?

_____

_____

 Notes for Home: Your child learned about the French and Indian War, Lord Dunmore's War, and colonists' growing conflicts with the American Indians.
Home Activity: Discuss with your child how to look at the French and Indian War from different points of view, including that of the French, the British, the colonists, and the American Indians.

© Scott Foresman 4 VA

Name _____ Date _____

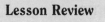

Lesson 3: Trouble with Britain

Directions: Read each of the following sentences. If the sentence is true, write *true* on the line to the left of the sentence. Then write one more detail about the topic of the sentence on the lines below it. If the sentence is false, write *false*. Then rewrite the sentence so that it makes a true statement. You may use your textbook.

_____ 1. The Committee of Correspondence was a statement objecting to the Stamp Act.

_____

_____

_____

_____ 2. The Boston Tea Party was a protest over a tax on tea.

_____

_____

_____

_____ 3. The First Continental Congress was a meeting of twelve colonies in which the delegates agreed to ban trade with Great Britain.

_____

_____

_____

_____ 4. The Virginia Resolves was a group set up to alert other colonies when one colony had trouble with Great Britain.

_____

_____

_____

_____ 5. Patrick Henry is known for delivering a fiery speech criticizing colonists for boycotting British goods.

_____

_____

_____

 Notes for Home: Your child learned about the growing tension between the American colonies and Great Britain.
Home Activity: With your child, identify some of the places discussed in this lesson on a world map. Places to identify include Great Britain, Boston, and Philadelphia.

© Scott Foresman 4 VA

Use with Pages 208–209.

Compare Line and Bar Graphs

Directions: Graphs show information about numbers in a way that is easy to understand. A line graph shows the relationship between sets of facts. A bar graph compares different items. Look at the line graph to the right and the bar graph to the left. Then answer the questions that follow on the lines provided.

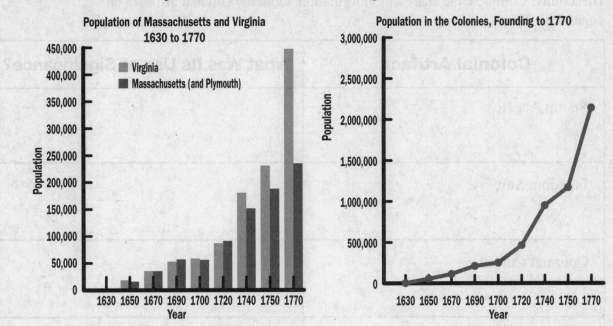

1. Which graph compares the population in two colonies? Which shows how the population in all the colonies grew over a period of time?

   _____

   _____

   _____

2. In what year did the population in all the colonies reach over one million people?

   _____

3. About how many people lived in all the colonies by 1770?

   _____

4. Which colony, Massachusetts or Virginia, had more people in 1770?

   _____

Notes for Home: Your child learned to read and compare line and bar graphs.
Home Activity: Find a line or bar graph in a newspaper or magazine. Read the graph with your child, identifying what each axis represents.

© Scott Foresman 4 VA

Colonial Artifacts

Colonists made good use of the natural resources of eastern North America. As the colonies became more self-sufficient, colonists became less dependent on Great Britain for goods.

Directions: Complete the chart with information about the colonial artifacts on pages 210–211.

Colonial Artifact	What Was Its Use or Significance?
Stamp Act Box	
Freedom Suit	
Colonial Currency	
A Silversmith's Tools and Products	
Household Gadgets	

Directions: In the space below, design a colonial artifact that could have been made using a natural resource of eastern North America. Tell your classmates about your artifact and explain how it helped the colonies become more self-sufficient.

Notes for Home: Your child learned how the colonists became less dependent on Great Britain as they made use of the natural resources of eastern North America.
Home Activity: With your child, discuss why economic independence was important to the American Revolution and how life might be different today if the colonies had not become self-sufficient.

Vocabulary Review

Directions: These are the vocabulary words from Chapter 7. How much do you know about these words? Use these words to complete the crossword puzzle. You may use your textbook.

capital	ally	boycott
immigrant	tax	congress
treaty	Parliament	militia

Across

3. money a government collects from its people

5. Great Britain's lawmaking body

6. a person or group that helps another reach a common goal

7. army made up of ordinary citizens who can be called together in an emergency

8. refuse to buy

Down

1. formal meeting

2. a city that serves as the home of a government

4. someone who moves to one country from another

9. formal agreement between two nations

Notes for Home: Your child learned the vocabulary words from Chapter 7.
Home Activity: Take turns with your child using the vocabulary words in complete sentences. Encourage your child to form sentences about the growing tension between the colonies and Great Britain.

Name _____ Date _____

UNIT 3 Project This Just In

Directions: Report breaking news in Virginia's history. In a group, choose an important event in Virginia's history. Then report the event in a press conference.

1. The event that we chose is _____.

2. My role in the press conference is (✔ one)

   _____ news reporter   _____ official or expert   _____ other participant

3. Here are some details about the event:

   What happened: _____

   Where and when the event took place: _____

   Who was involved: _____

   Result or importance of the event: _____

4. Here are some questions and answers that we will ask and answer in our press conference:

   News reporter: _____

   Official or expert: _____

   News reporter: _____

   Other participant: _____

✔ Checklist for Students

_____ We chose an event in Virginia's history.

_____ We found information about the event.

_____ We wrote questions and answers about the event.

_____ We made a poster about the event to use in our press conference.

_____ We presented our press conference to the class.

Notes for Home: Your child learned how to report important details of an event in a press conference.
Home Activity: Watch a news program with your child. Discuss what important facts are reported about each event, and why the events might be important to the region where the events occurred.

© Scott Foresman 4 VA

Workbook

Compare and Contrast

Directions: Comparing two or more things means finding ways they are alike. Contrasting two or more things means finding ways they are different. Fill in the circle next to the correct answer. You may use your textbook.

1. Which of the following does NOT signal a comparison between two or more things?

   Ⓐ both
   Ⓑ as well as
   Ⓒ on the other hand
   Ⓓ like

2. Which of the following signals a contrast between two or more things?

   Ⓐ both
   Ⓑ unlike
   Ⓒ like
   Ⓓ as well as

3. Which of the following makes a comparison?

   Ⓐ The American Revolution brought about changes in government as well as for the colonists.
   Ⓑ Royal governors ruled Virginia, unlike after the American Revolution.
   Ⓒ Burgesses tried to win fair treatment for the colonists. But their power was limited.
   Ⓓ Great Britain had tried to rule Virginia, but Virginia was now part of the United States.

4. Which of the following contrasts two or more things?

   Ⓐ Both the British and the colonists wanted to govern Virginia.
   Ⓑ Like the British, the colonists sought to control resources.
   Ⓒ Colonists believed that they had complaints against the British government as well as against Lord Dunmore.
   Ⓓ Unlike the people in the colonies, Great Britain had the power of an empire.

5. Which of the following best describes government in Virginia before the Revolution and after?

   Ⓐ Unlike before the Revolution, Virginia no longer followed Great Britain's laws.
   Ⓑ Virginia's voters still elected burgesses the same as before the Revolution.
   Ⓒ Royal governors ruled Virginia. However, after the war, the voters of Virginia helped make their own laws.
   Ⓓ The House of Burgesses did not have much power. On the other hand, the burgesses tried to win fair treatment for the colonists.

Notes for Home: Your child learned how to identify words that signal comparisons and contrasts and how to compare and contrast two or more ideas in a passage.
Home Activity: Read an editorial column from a newspaper with your child. Together, identify words that signal comparisons and contrasts. Then compare and contrast two or more different ideas about a local issue or event.

Name _____ Date _____

Vocabulary Preview

Directions: These are the vocabulary words from Chapter 8. How much do you know about these words? Match each vocabulary word to its meaning. Write the number of the word on the blank next to its meaning. You may use your textbook.

1. Loyalist   _____ a document that states the basic laws and rules of a government

2. Patriot   _____ a colonist who opposed the British

3. convention   _____ a troop of soldiers on horses

4. constitution   _____ a colonist loyal to the British

5. cavalry   _____ a large meeting of members of a group for a common purpose

Directions: Choose the vocabulary word from above that best completes each sentence. Write the word on the line provided.

6. The colonist did not want to fight against the British because he was a true

   _____.

7. He believed in freedom from the British government, so he called himself a

   _____.

8. People from all over the colony met at the _____ in Williamsburg.

9. To find out about a state's rules and laws, you can read its _____.

10. The members of a _____ rode by quickly on tall horses.

Notes for Home: Your child learned the vocabulary terms for Chapter 8.
Home Activity: Practice saying, spelling, and using these words correctly with your child.

© Scott Foresman 4 VA

Lesson 1: Early Struggles

Directions: Conflicts between the colonists and the British continued to grow and led to fighting in Virginia. Sequence the events in the order in which they took place by numbering them from 1–10. You may use your textbook.

_____ 1. The Patriots defeated the British near Norfolk at Great Bridge.

_____ 2. Patriot soldiers forced Dunmore onto Gwynn's Island.

_____ 3. Patrick Henry demanded that Lord Dunmore return the gunpowder or pay for it.

_____ 4. Finally, Dunmore gave up and left Virginia for good.

_____ 5. Lord Dunmore fled to Norfolk because he no longer felt safe in Williamsburg.

_____ 6. Dunmore regained control of Norfolk for a short time.

_____ 7. Lord Dunmore took Williamsburg's supply of gunpowder.

_____ 8. The Second Continental Congress elected George Washington to command the Continental Army.

_____ 9. After losing at Great Bridge, Dunmore bombarded Norfolk with cannon balls.

_____ 10. The colonists began to raise a real army and increase the size of the militia.

Notes for Home: Your child learned about the growing conflict between the colonists and the British and the sequence of events that led to the battle at Great Bridge.
Home Activity: Review with your child the sequence of events in this lesson. Then have your child summarize what happened.

© Scott Foresman 4 VA

Name _____ Date _____

Lesson 2: Independence

Directions: In 1776 the Virginia Convention influenced important written documents. Complete the chart with information from this lesson. Then answer the questions that follow. You may use your textbook.

Important Documents of 1776	
Document	**What did the document state?**
Virginia Declaration of Rights	
Virginia constitution	
Declaration of Independence	

1. How did George Mason's ideas in the Virginia Declaration of Rights influence the Declaration of Independence?

_____

_____

2. Who wrote the Declaration of Independence? For whom was it written?

_____

_____

Notes for Home: Your child learned how Virginia and the Second Continental Congress declared independence from Great Britain.
Home Activity: Review with your child the concepts of freedom and independence and how they are central to the three major documents of 1776. Also reinforce how the powerful ideas contained in the Virginia Declaration of Rights serve as the foundation for ideas expressed in the Virginia constitution and in the Declaration of Independence.

Lesson 3: Battlefield Virginia

Directions: Virginians served in many ways during the Revolutionary War, finally defeating the British. Answer the following questions on the lines provided. You may use your textbook.

1. Give three examples of Virginians' contributions during the Revolutionary War.

_____

_____

_____

_____

2. What were the strengths of the Continental Army?

_____

_____

3. Why did Virginia decide to move its capital from Williamsburg to Richmond?

_____

_____

_____

4. Why did leaders of the Virginia government meet in Charlottesville and then in Staunton in 1781?

_____

_____

5. Summarize what happened at Yorktown.

_____

_____

_____

Directions: Imagine you are one of the Virginians mentioned in this lesson. On a separate sheet of paper, write a letter to a friend. Tell your friend about your experiences in the Revolutionary War and how you helped the Continental Army.

Notes for Home: Your child learned about the ways in which Virginians contributed to the colonists' victory during the Revolutionary War.
Home Activity: Review the various contributions made by Virginians. Use the examples to discuss the concepts of determination, sacrifice, and bravery.

© Scott Foresman 4 VA

Use Primary and Secondary Sources

Directions: A *primary source* is an eyewitness account of history. A *secondary source* is a secondhand account of history. Both kinds of sources provide useful information about history. Answer the following questions about primary and secondary sources.

1. From what point of view are primary sources written?

   _____

   _____

2. From what point of view are secondary sources written?

   _____

   _____

3. What are two examples of primary sources and two examples of secondary sources?

   _____

   _____

   _____

4. Suppose you wanted to read a single book about the importance of the victory at Yorktown. Explain what kind of source might be most helpful.

   _____

   _____

   _____

5. Suppose you wanted to read the words of James Armistead describing his experiences as a spy. What kind of source do you think might be most helpful? Explain.

   _____

   _____

   _____

© Scott Foresman 4 VA

Notes for Home: Your child learned how to distinguish between and use primary and secondary sources in their research and writing.
Home Activity: With your child, read portions of the diary or memoirs of a key figure in history. Discuss how a primary source helps us understand how real people thought, felt, and acted at a particular time and place.

Vocabulary Review

Directions: Use each of the vocabulary terms from Chapter 8 in a sentence. Include details from the lesson in your sentences. Write the sentences on the lines provided. You may use your glossary.

1. Loyalist

_____

_____

_____

2. Patriot

_____

_____

_____

3. convention

_____

_____

_____

4. constitution

_____

_____

_____

5. cavalry

_____

_____

_____

Notes for Home: Your child learned the vocabulary terms for Chapter 8.
Home Activity: Discuss the vocabulary terms and how they relate to the American Revolution.

© Scott Foresman 4 VA

Name _____ Date _____

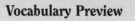

Vocabulary Preview

Directions: These are the vocabulary words from Chapter 9. How much do you know about these words? Match each vocabulary word to its meaning. Write the number of the word on the blank next to its meaning. You may use your textbook.

1. compromise   _____ adopt formally

2. amend   _____ a person who wanted to end slavery

3. ratify   _____ change

4. dynasty   _____ a machine that cleans cotton

5. cotton gin   _____ when two sides each give up some demands

6. abolitionist   _____ a line of people or groups that holds power for a long time

Directions: Locate the vocabulary words in the word puzzle below.

A	B	O	L	I	T	I	O	N	I	S	T
M	J	Y	N	T	A	P	Q	E	M	B	L
E	A	R	A	T	I	F	Y	H	L	K	V
N	H	C	E	Q	S	L	P	V	L	D	D
D	Y	N	A	S	T	Y	S	J	F	E	B
V	C	Z	C	O	T	T	O	N	G	I	N
C	Q	T	U	L	W	J	L	Z	C	O	A
D	C	O	M	P	R	O	M	I	S	E	T

Notes for Home: Your child learned the vocabulary terms for Chapter 9.
Home Activity: Practice saying, spelling, and using these words correctly with your child.

© Scott Foresman 4 VA

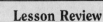
Lesson 1: A Plan for Government

Directions: The Continental Congress developed a plan for a government of the new United States. Use the terms in the box to complete each sentence with information from Lesson 1. You may use your textbook.

Articles of Confederation	Bill of Rights
Virginia Plan	Annapolis, Maryland
James Madison	Philadelphia, Pennsylvania
Great Compromise	

1. The agreement for a two-house legislature came about because of the

    _____.

2. The ten amendments to the Constitution are known as the

    _____.

3. The Continental Congress wrote the _____,

    which was a plan for a government of the new United States.

4. A small group of state leaders met in _____ to

    discuss the future of the new United States; a larger convention was then scheduled for

    May of 1787 in _____.

5. Virginian _____ felt that the state needed a

    strong central government; his ideas formed a big part of what was called the

    _____.

Notes for Home: Your child learned about the Continental Congress's plan for a government of the new United States.
Home Activity: Spend time discussing with your child the importance of this plan.

Lesson 2: The Virginia Dynasty

Directions: Write the number of each item in Column A on the blank next to its example or description in Column B.

Column A	Column B
1. Louisiana Purchase	_____ played a key role in her husband's presidency
2. Lewis and Clark Expedition	_____ became the basis for the First Amendment to the Constitution
3. Sacagawea	_____ an informative journey from the Mississippi River to the Pacific coast
4. Dolley Madison	_____ James Monroe's two peaceful terms as President
5. War of 1812	_____ where the British were defeated during the War of 1812
6. Virginia Statute for Religious Freedom	_____ Shoshone woman who guided Lewis and Clark
7. Meriwether Lewis and William Clark	_____ two Virginians sent by Thomas Jefferson on a great expedition
8. Era of Good Feeling	_____ caused by Britain's refusal to give up forts in the Northwest Territory
9. Monroe Doctrine	_____ large area of land bought by Thomas Jefferson from France
10. Craney Island	_____ a policy that warned other nations not to interfere in North and South American countries

© Scott Foresman 4 VA

Notes for Home: Your child learned about the contributions of the Virginians who led the nation during the years 1789 to 1825.
Home Activity: Review with your child some of the major contributions made by Virginians, such as James Monroe's policy known as the Monroe Doctrine. Explain that this policy still plays a key role in our government today.

Name _____ Date _____

Lesson 3: The Issue of Slavery

Directions: The practice of slavery divided Virginians and the nation. Answer the questions below about slavery in Virginia and elsewhere in the country. You may use your textbook.

1. What factors contributed to the widespread practice of slavery in the South?

_____

_____

_____

2. What effect did Eli Whitney's cotton gin have on slavery?

_____

_____

_____

3. What was the Underground Railroad? Who was Harriet Tubman?

The underground railroad was a bunch of routes and tunnels. Harriet Tubman worked on it.

4. How did Virginians react to Nat Turner's rebellion in Southampton County?

Virginians reacted by making laws that stopped slaves from gathering or walking freely.

5. Why did John Brown's actions at Harpers Ferry raise tensions between the North and South about slavery?

The north didn't like his violent ways the south thought his action about abolishanists counted him a hero

Notes for Home: Your child learned about the practice of slavery and how it divided Virginians and the nation.
Home Activity: Review with your child the series of events that increased the demand for slavery and eventually led to heightened tensions between the North and South.

Name _____ Date _____

Use a Road Map

Directions: A road map shows the roads and streets in an area. It can also show important buildings, parks, waterways, and other landmarks. The map on this page shows the capital of Virginia, Richmond. Read the map and answer the questions that follow.

Richmond

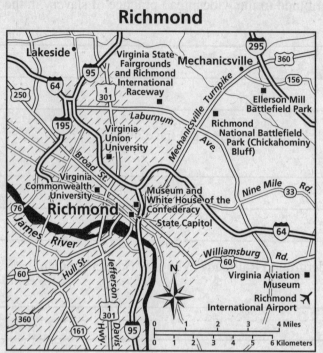

1. About how far is Lakeside from the center of Richmond?

   _____

2. In which direction would you drive to get from Virginia Commonwealth University to Richmond International Airport?

   _____

3. From the center of Richmond, what is the name of the turnpike you would take to Richmond National Battlefield Park and Ellerson Mill Battlefield Park?

   _____

4. What major river flows through Richmond?

   _____

5. Which roads could you take to enter Richmond from the southwest?

   _____

Notes for Home: Your child learned how to read a road map.
Home Activity: Find a road map of your city or town. Work with your child to locate familiar roads and streets, buildings, parks, and other landmarks of your area.

Vocabulary Review

Directions: Write each vocabulary word from Chapter 9 beside its description.
Then pretend that you are one of the following people: James Madison, Dolley
Madison, or James Monroe. Write a diary entry about the new nation. Use four
vocabulary words in your diary entry to describe the creation of a new government
and some of the struggles the new nation faced.

_____ **1.** a machine that cleans cotton

_____ **2.** adopt formally

_____ **3.** when two sides each give up some demands

_____ **4.** a person who wanted to end slavery

_____ **5.** a line of people or groups that holds power for a long time

_____ **6.** change

Diary Entry:

_____

_____

_____

_____

_____

_____

_____

_____

_____

_____

Notes for Home: Your child learned the vocabulary terms for Chapter 9.
Home Activity: Read aloud the diary entry your child wrote. Discuss the vocabulary terms he or she used.

© Scott Foresman 4 VA

Name _____ Date _____

UNIT
4 Project **Point of View**

In a group, choose a topic from this unit that was important to the history of Virginia. Then take sides and debate your topic for the class.

1. The topic we chose is _____.

2. Below are the two sides of the topic we decided to argue. The (✔) shows the side I will argue:

_____ Side A _____

_____ Side B _____

3. Facts supporting Side A:

_____

_____

4. Facts supporting Side B:

_____

_____

✔**Checklist for Students**
_____ We chose a topic that was important to the history of Virginia.
_____ We found information on the issue.
_____ We gathered facts to support opposing sides of the issue.
_____ We shared what we learned by presenting a debate in class.

Notes for Home: Your child learned to debate a topic that was important to Virginia's history.
Home Activity: Read one of the "letters to the editor" in your local newspaper with your child. Then discuss some different points of view other people may have on the subject.

Draw Conclusions

Directions: A conclusion is a judgment that a person reaches using information.
Fill in the circle next to the correct answer. You may use page 289 of your textbook.

1. When the Civil War began, the South and the North each had strengths and weaknesses.
   Which of the following does NOT help you draw this conclusion?

   Ⓐ The North had a more powerful navy.

   Ⓑ The South had many top military leaders.

   Ⓒ Both sides believed the war would end quickly.

   Ⓓ The North had more factories to help supply troops.

2. The North had more factories and more miles of railroads than the Southern states. What
   conclusion might you draw from this information?

   Ⓐ The North had many weaknesses.

   Ⓑ The North would win important battlefield victories.

   Ⓒ The North would be able to defeat leaders loyal to the South.

   Ⓓ The North would be able to keep its troops better supplied.

3. The North had a much more powerful navy than the South had. What conclusion might
   you draw from this information?

   Ⓐ The South thought it could win the war.

   Ⓑ The North and South were evenly matched for sea battles.

   Ⓒ The North did not have strong supply routes.

   Ⓓ The North had an advantage because it could control the seas.

4. The South had many strengths at the beginning of the Civil War. Which of the following
   does NOT help you draw this conclusion?

   Ⓐ Robert E. Lee was a great leader.

   Ⓑ The North had more factories and more railroads.

   Ⓒ The South needed only to win some important battles.

   Ⓓ Many believed the North would accept the South's independence.

5. The North had many strengths at the beginning of the Civil War. Which of the following
   does NOT help you draw this conclusion?

   Ⓐ Great leaders, such as Robert E. Lee, were loyal to the South.

   Ⓑ Far more people lived in the North than in the South.

   Ⓒ The North's navy had almost full control of the seas.

   Ⓓ The North had more factories.

Notes for Home: Your child learned how to draw conclusions from information presented in a text.
Home Activity: Read a news or sports article from a newspaper with your child. Together, identify
information that the writer presents and what conclusions have been drawn. If the writer does not draw a
conclusion, discuss with your child what conclusion can be made based on the information in the article.
It may be helpful to review the article and underline specific facts and details that will help your child draw
a conclusion.

© Scott Foresman 4 VA

Vocabulary Preview

Directions: These are the vocabulary words from Chapter 10. How much do you know about these words? Choose the vocabulary from the box that best completes each sentence. Write the word on the line provided. You may use your textbook.

secede	emancipate
blockade	surrender

1. A closing off of an area so that people and supplies cannot get in or out is called a

   _____.

2. To set free means to _____.

3. To give up means to _____.

4. To formally withdraw from a group means to _____.

Directions: Use each of the vocabulary words in a sentence. Write the sentence on the line provided.

5. secede

   _____

   _____

6. blockade

   _____

   _____

7. emancipate

   _____

   _____

8. surrender

   _____

   _____

Notes for Home: Your child learned the vocabulary terms for Chapter 10.
Home Activity: Review the vocabulary words with your child. Have your child use each of the vocabulary words in a new sentence. Together, find an example that describes or illustrates the meaning of each word. For example: Lee had no choice but to surrender, or give up.

© Scott Foresman 4 VA

Lesson 1: The Nation Breaks Apart

Directions: After much debate, Virginia joined other states that had seceded from the United States. Draw a line from each item in column A to its description in column B.

Column A	Column B
1. Abraham Lincoln	a. a Virginian who was among the first to fire shots at Fort Sumter
2. Jefferson Davis	b. the states that seceded from the United States
3. Edmund Ruffin	c. the commander of Virginia's military forces
4. Winfield Scott	d. an army officer from Virginia who remained loyal to the Union
5. Robert E. Lee	e. the United States
6. Union	f. the president of the Confederate States
7. Confederate States of America	g. the President of the United States

Directions: Answer the following questions on the lines provided.

8. Why did the presidential election of 1860 add to the tensions between the North and South?

   He was against slavery

9. Why was Virginia reluctant to secede from the Union?

   They didn't want wer

10. What events at Fort Sumter led to the start of the Civil War?

    They were fighting

Notes for Home: Your child learned about the secession of many states from the Union and the events that led to the start of the Civil War.
Home Activity: Review with your child the reasons why some states wanted to break off from the United States. Ask your child to describe the events that led to the firing of the first shots of the Civil War.

Lesson 2: Early Victories

Directions: The Confederates had some successes and setbacks in the early battles of the Civil War. Complete the chart with a summary about each battle. Then answer the question that follows. You may use your textbook.

Battle	Summary of What Happened
1. First Manassas (First Battle of Bull Run)	
2. Seven Days' Battle	
3. Second Manassas (Second Battle of Bull Run)	
4. Battle of Sharpsburg (Antietam)	

5. How did the Emancipation Proclamation help the Union?

_____

_____

_____

Notes for Home: Your child learned about the early battles of the Civil War.
Home Activity: Review the different battles with your child. Using a map, locate the different battle sites.

© Scott Foresman 4 VA

Name _____ Date _____

Lesson 3: The War Ends

Directions: Confederate forces fought well but finally surrendered to the Union. Answer the following questions on the lines provided. You may use your textbook.

1. Why did General Lee decide to march his troops into Gettysburg in 1863?

   _____

   _____

2. What happened at Gettysburg?

   _____

   _____

   _____

3. What was important about the Union's victory at Vicksburg, Mississippi?

   _____

   _____

4. What was the condition of Lee's army by the spring of 1865?

   _____

   _____

5. Summarize what happened at Appomattox Court House.

   _____

   _____

   _____

Directions: Imagine you are a soldier in Lee's army at the end of the war in the spring of 1865. On a separate sheet of paper, write a letter to a family member or to a friend. Describe what you think of the two generals—Lee and Grant. Why do you have great respect for both generals?

© Scott Foresman 4 VA

Notes for Home: Your child learned about the battles that led to Lee's surrender and the end of the Civil War. **Home Activity:** Review the way in which the war ended at Appomattox Court House. Discuss the idea of respect. Point out the respect that Lee and Grant had for each other. Discuss how Grant showed that respect to the defeated Lee and to Confederate soldiers.

Use a Cross-Section Diagram

Directions: A *cross-section* is a special type of drawing or diagram. It shows what an object would look like it if were cut in half. Look at the cross-section diagram below and answer the questions.

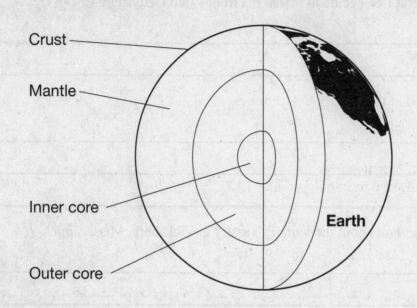

Crust

Mantle

Inner core

Outer core

Earth

1. What does the cross-section diagram of Earth let you see?

_____

2. What different parts of our planet are shown in the diagram?

_____

3. How much of Earth is normally hidden from our view?

_____

4. Use the diagram to describe the positions of the different layers of Earth.

_____

_____

5. Why might this view of our planet be helpful to people?

_____

_____

Notes for Home: Your child learned how to use a cross-section diagram to show what an object would look like it if were cut in half.
Home Activity: With your child, select an ordinary object, such as a pencil, or a fruit or vegetable, such as a tomato or green pepper. Cut the object in half. Together, closely look at the object and identify the different layers and parts. Then have your child create a cross-section diagram, using the object as a model.

Vocabulary Review

Directions: Match each vocabulary word to its meaning. Write the letter of the word on the blank next to its meaning.

_____ 1. to set free   **a.** secede

_____ 2. to give up   **b.** blockade

_____ 3. to withdraw formally from a group   **c.** emancipate

_____ 4. a closing off of an area so that people
and supplies cannot get in or out   **d.** surrender

Directions: Write a letter to a friend. Tell your friend about the end of the Civil War. Use each vocabulary word once in your letter.

Dear _____ ,

_____

_____

_____

_____

_____

_____

_____

_____

_____

_____

Your friend,

_____

Notes for Home: Your child learned the vocabulary terms for Chapter 10.
Home Activity: Discuss the vocabulary terms and how they relate to the Civil War.

© Scott Foresman 4 VA

Vocabulary Preview

Directions: These are the vocabulary words from Chapter 11. How much do you know about these words? Draw a line from each word to its meaning. You may use your glossary.

1. sharecropping   **a.** the right to vote

2. suffrage   **b.** a variety of people of different races, religions, and backgrounds

3. discrimination   **c.** the separation of African Americans and white people

4. segregation   **d.** an unfair difference in the treatment of people

5. diversity   **e.** a system of farming in which a landowner provides workers with land, seeds, and equipment in return for a share of the crop

Directions: Practice using each word in a sentence.

1. sharecropping

_____

_____

2. suffrage

_____

_____

3. discrimination

_____

_____

4. segregation

_____

_____

5. diversity

_____

_____

Notes for Home: Your child learned the vocabulary terms for Chapter 11.
Home Activity: Practice saying, spelling, and using these words correctly with your child.

© Scott Foresman 4 VA

Lesson 1: Virginia Faces the Future

Directions: Virginians faced many challenges as they tried to rebuild their state and rejoin the Union. Explain each term below on the lines provided. You may use your textbook.

1. Freedmen's Bureau

_____

_____

_____

2. sharecropping

_____

_____

_____

_____

3. Reconstruction

_____

_____

_____

_____

4. Radicals

_____

_____

_____

5. Black Codes

_____

_____

_____

© Scott Foresman 4 VA

Notes for Home: Your child learned about the challenges Virginians faced as they looked to the future after the Civil War.
Home Activity: Review with your child the reasons why Virginians faced so many challenges after the Civil War.

Use Newspapers and the Internet

Directions: Newspapers offer a lot of information about history and current events. Newspapers contain several different kinds of stories. The Internet also provides a lot of information. The Internet is a huge network of computers that contains many Web sites. Answer the following questions on the lines provided. You may use your textbook.

1. What is the difference between the kind of information presented by current newspapers and historic newspapers?

   _____

   _____

   _____

2. How is the information in newspapers organized?

   _____

   _____

   _____

3. Explain the two basic ways you can look for information on the Internet.

   _____

   _____

   _____

4. What does a search engine do?

   _____

   _____

   _____

5. Which Web sites often have more dependable information than other sites?

   _____

   _____

   _____

Notes for Home: Your child learned how to use historic and current newspapers and the Internet to find information.
Home Activity: With your child, read a current issue of your local newspaper. Review the different headlines and articles. Then select one article of interest. Ask your child what keywords he or she would use to find more information about the topic on the Internet.

© Scott Foresman 4 VA

Lesson 2: African American Rights

Directions: African Americans gained many rights after the Civil War but lost some of those rights by the end of the 1800s. Complete the outline with information from the textbook.

African Americans After the Civil War

I. African Americans Gain Rights

   A. Enslaved African Americans gained their freedom after the war.

   B. African American men won _____—the right to vote.

      1. They used their votes to win seats in the _____.

      2. _____ was the first African American from Virginia elected to the United States Congress.

      3. African American voters helped elect leaders who got rid of the

      _____.

II. African Americans Lose Rights

   A. Many white Virginians did not like the growing power of African Americans. Discrimination against African Americans became worse.

   B. New laws led to the loss of rights.

      1. Virginians met to write a new constitution; they wanted to make it harder for

      African Americans to _____.

      2. A system of laws called _____ was designed to separate African Americans and whites.

III. African Americans Help Themselves

   A. _____ used his Richmond newspaper to report on the poor treatment of African Americans.

   B. Lawyer _____ fought against the Jim Crow laws.

   C. Teacher _____ worked to improve Virginia's African American schools.

   D. Senator _____ supported giving land in the West to African American settlers.

Notes for Home: Your child learned about the rights African Americans gained and lost after the Civil War. **Home Activity:** Discuss the concept of discrimination with your child. Explain how many laws, such as Jim Crow laws, that discriminated against African Americans were still in effect in the South in the 1950s and 1960s. Explain that during the 1960s African Americans had to fight again for their rights.

Name _____ Date _____

Lesson Review

Use with Pages 338–344.

Lesson 3: A New Economy

Directions: Virginia's economy grew stronger in the late 1800s. Answer the
questions about why life improved for many people in Virginia in the late 1800s and
early 1900s. You may use your textbook.

1. What changes did the railroads bring to many towns in Virginia?

   _____

   _____

   _____

   _____

2. How did Newport News become one of the world's great shipyards?

   _____

   _____

   _____

3. In the late 1800s, what kinds of products were produced in Virginia and shipped all over
   the world?

   _____

   _____

4. How did the growth of railroads benefit farmers in Virginia?

   _____

   _____

5. How did the invention of the refrigerated railroad car help farmers make more money?

   _____

   _____

   _____

   _____

   _____

Notes for Home: Your child learned about Virginia's growing economy in the late 1800s and the positive
impact that had on life for many Virginians.
Home Activity: Discuss with your child the role transportation, industry, and agriculture play in our
economy today.

78 Lesson Review

Workbook

Vocabulary Review

Directions: Use the vocabulary words from Chapter 11 to complete the crossword puzzle.

Across

3. an unfair difference in the treatment of people

5. a variety of people of different races, religions, and backgrounds

Down

1. a system of farming in which the landowner provides land, seed, and equipment to workers

2. the right to vote

4. a system of laws designed to separate African Americans and white people

Notes for Home: Your child learned the vocabulary terms for Chapter 11.
Home Activity: Take turns with your child using each of the terms in this chapter in complete sentences.

© Scott Foresman 4 VA

Use with Page 352.

UNIT
5 Project   Ad Sales

In a group, choose a product or business. Then plan an infomercial about the product or business.

1. The product or business we chose is _____.

2. Below is some information about our product or business. The (✔) shows my role in the infomercial.

_____ **Business or product representative:** Describe the product or business, its history, and its value or cost.

_____

_____ **Satisfied customer:** Tell about your experience with the product or business and why you recommend it.

_____

_____ **Local resident or official:** Tell how the product or business contributes to the economy.

_____

_____ **Expert:** Explain why the product or business is better than its competitors.

_____

✔**Checklist for Students**

_____ We chose a product or business.

_____ We found information about our product or business.

_____ We wrote a script for our infomercial.

_____ We made a poster or banner to use in our infomercial.

_____ We presented our infomercial to the class.

Notes for Home: Your child researched a product or business and helped present an infomercial to the class.
Home Activity: Watch an infomercial or commercial with your child. Discuss the advertiser's sales techniques and strategies. Talk about how the advertised business or product benefits the economy.

Summarize

Directions: Read the article "Challenges in a New Century" on page 359. Then fill in the circle next to the correct answer.

1. Which statement is the best summary of the article?

   Ⓐ The 1900s in the United States were challenging years.
   Ⓑ War helped bring prosperity back to the United States.
   Ⓒ Great hope and challenges marked the 1900s in the United States.
   Ⓓ The good times ended with the Great Depression in 1929.

2. Which sentence would NOT be part of a summary of this article?

   Ⓐ European countries bought many supplies from the United States.
   Ⓑ The twentieth century in the United States began with promise and struggle.
   Ⓒ During the Great Depression, businesses closed and banks failed.
   Ⓓ After Germany attacked U.S. ships, America joined in the war.

3. Which answer best summarizes the second paragraph?

   Ⓐ World War I began in 1914. During the war, business improved in the United States.
   Ⓑ War erupted in Europe in 1914. The United States stayed out of the war until Germany attacked U.S. ships. Soon after, the United States joined the war in Europe.
   Ⓒ In 1914 the war in Europe started. America joined the battle and sent soldiers to fight in Europe.
   Ⓓ The war began in Europe in 1914. The United States tried not to take sides in the war. Many Americans didn't want to become involved in the European war. At first, the war improved business in the United States.

4. Which answer best summarizes the third paragraph?

   Ⓐ The Great Depression brought hunger and despair. People could not find jobs. They lost their farms and homes.
   Ⓑ After World War II, prosperity returned to the United States. The good times ended with the Great Depression in 1929.
   Ⓒ In 1929 many businesses, farms, and banks failed. This difficult time period is known as the Great Depression.
   Ⓓ After the war, the United States enjoyed a period of good times that ended in 1929 with the Great Depression. The Great Depression was a difficult period for many people and businesses.

Notes for Home: Your child learned to summarize information from a text.
Home Activity: Read a brief article with your child. Ask him or her to summarize what you read. Make sure your child's summary includes the main ideas from the article.

Vocabulary Preview

Directions: These are the vocabulary words from Chapter 12. How much do you know about these words? Choose the vocabulary from the box that best completes each sentence. Write the word on the line provided. You may use your textbook.

suffragist	desegregation
neutral	integration
depression	civil rights

1. The equal inclusion of people of all races is known as _____.

2. Rights that the United States Constitution promises all citizens are called

   _____.

3. The process of ending segregation, or the separating of people by race, is known as

   _____.

4. A person working to win the right to vote is called a _____.

5. A time of little business activity is called a _____.

6. Not taking sides means to be _____.

Notes for Home: Your child learned the vocabulary terms for Chapter 12.
Home Activity: Review the vocabulary words with your child. Have your child use each of the vocabulary words in a new sentence. Together, find an example in the chapter that describes or illustrates the meaning of each word. For example: In 1920, the Nineteenth Amendment to the United States gave women suffrage.

Lesson 1: Virginia's New Leaders

Directions: In the early 1900s, new leaders emerged to guide Virginia and the nation. Answer the following questions on the lines provided.

1. What contributions did President Woodrow Wilson make to the United States?

_____

_____

_____

_____

2. Explain Harry Flood Byrd, Sr.'s, "pay-as-you-go" plan. How did it benefit Virginia?

_____

_____

_____

_____

3. What contributions did Byrd make while he was governor of Virginia?

_____

_____

_____

_____

4. What contributions did women in Virginia make to public life before they won the right to vote?

_____

_____

_____

_____

5. For what are Anne Clay Crenshaw, Lila Mead Valentine, and Ellen Glasgow known?

_____

_____

_____

_____

Notes for Home: Your child learned about new leaders who emerged in the 1900s and about their contributions to Virginia and the nation.
Home Activity: Review with your child the different accomplishments and contributions made by Virginia's new leaders.

© Scott Foresman 4 VA

Lesson 2: Time of Conflict and Crisis

Directions: Two world wars and a terrible depression brought great change and growth to Virginia. Complete the outline with information from the textbook.

Changes and Growth in Virginia

I. World War I

  A. The war gave a big boost to businesses in Virginia.

    1. As businesses grew, so did Virginia's _____.

    2. The city of _____ became a center for making ammunition and chemicals.

  B. Virginians made many sacrifices.

    1. Many joined the _____, including women.

    2. Many Virginians moved from farms to cities to work in

    _____ and shipyards.

II. Great Depression

  A. During the depression that began in 1929, workers lost their _____,

  and many families went _____ and hungry.

  B. State and federal governments tried to help people hurt by the Great Depression.

    1. Franklin Delano Roosevelt's ideas became known as the _____.

    2. Harry Flood Byrd, Sr.'s, _____ plan helped keep Virginia out of debt.

III. World War II

  A. The United States entered the war after Japanese planes bombed the U.S. naval base at

  _____.

  B. The war brought an end to the Great Depression. There were jobs for everyone.

    1. Factories geared up to supply the troops.

    2. Between 1941 and 1943, workers built the _____ in Arlington, which served as headquarters for the United States military.

Notes for Home: Your child learned about the growth and changes that occurred in Virginia after World Wars I and II and the Great Depression.
Home Activity: Review with your child how events affected people in Virginia and in the United States.

© Scott Foresman 4 VA

Lesson 3: African Americans Win Rights

Directions: Explain each name or term and tell how it relates to African Americans'
struggle to win equal rights in the 1960s. You may use your textbook.

1. "separate but equal"

_____

_____

_____

_____

2. massive resistance and Prince Edward County

_____

_____

_____

_____

3. Carter G. Woodson

_____

_____

_____

_____

4. Dr. Martin Luther King, Jr.

_____

_____

_____

_____

5. Douglas Wilder

_____

_____

_____

_____

Notes for Home: Your child learned about African Americans' struggle for civil rights in America.
Home Activity: Discuss the concept of equality and how the U.S. Constitution and our government are
based on the concept of freedom and equality for all.

Read Vertical Time Lines

Directions: A time line is a way to organize historical events in order according to when they happened. A *vertical time line* runs from top to bottom. Look at the vertical time line below and answer the questions.

1914 — World War I erupts in Europe.

1917 — United States enters World War I.

1926 — Harry Flood Byrd, Sr., becomes governor of Virginia.

1929 — Great Depression begins.

1932 — Franklin Delano Roosevelt is elected President of the United States.

1941 — United States enters World War II.

1945 — World War II ends.

1. How many years are there between the time World War I began in Europe and the end of World War II?

_____

2. Was Franklin Delano Roosevelt elected President before or after the start of the Great Depression?

_____

3. How many years are there between the outbreak of World War I and the U.S. joining in the war?

_____

4. In what year was Harry Flood Byrd, Sr., elected governor of Virginia?

_____

5. World War II brought an end to the Great Depression. About how long did the Depression last?

_____

© Scott Foresman 4 VA

Notes for Home: Your child learned how to read a vertical time line.
Home Activity: With your child, create a vertical time line of important events in your child's life. Use the time line to reinforce your child's understanding of chronological order.

Vocabulary Review

Directions: Match each vocabulary word to its meaning. Write the letter of the word on the blank next to its meaning. Use each word in a sentence. Write the sentence on the lines provided underneath each word.

_____ 1. the equal inclusion of people of all races

_____ 2. a person working to win the right to vote

_____ 3. the process of ending segregation

_____ 4. a time of little business activity

_____ 5. not taking sides

_____ 6. rights that the U.S. Constitution promises all citizens

a. suffragist

_____

_____

b. neutral

_____

_____

c. depression

_____

_____

d. civil rights

_____

_____

e. integration

_____

_____

f. desegregation

_____

_____

Notes for Home: Your child learned the vocabulary terms for Chapter 12.
Home Activity: Discuss the vocabulary terms and how they relate to the conflicts and changes of the early twentieth century.

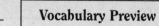
Vocabulary Preview

Directions: These are the vocabulary words from Chapter 13. How much do you know about these words? Draw a line from each word to its meaning. You may use your glossary.

1. manufacture   **a.** describing an area of high population density

2. budget   **b.** to make something, especially by machine

3. urban   **c.** a plan for state spending

Directions: Use each vocabulary word in a sentence. Write the sentence on the lines provided underneath each word.

4. manufacture

_____

_____

_____

_____

5. budget

_____

_____

_____

_____

6. urban

_____

_____

_____

_____

Notes for Home: Your child learned the vocabulary terms for Chapter 13.
Home Activity: Practice saying, spelling, and using these words correctly with your child.

Lesson 1: Virginians at Work

Directions: Many kinds of business and industry thrive in modern-day Virginia, and a great variety of products are made. Using information from this lesson, circle the term in parentheses that best completes each sentence.

1. Since Virginia's early years as a colony, (cotton, tobacco) has been an important cash crop.

2. Virginia's Cyrus McCormick invented the (McCormick loom, McCormick reaper),

   a machine that helped farmers harvest grain much faster than ever before.

3. Tobacco is grown mainly in the (Piedmont, Shenandoah Valley) and in southwestern Virginia.

4. Virginia is one of the country's biggest producers of (peanuts, apples).

5. Shipbuilding is centered in the (Piedmont, Tidewater) Region of Virginia.

6. One of the country's biggest (seaports, textile mills) is located in the Hampton Roads area

   of Newport News, Norfolk, and Portsmouth.

7. Many Virginians work in (seaports, coal mines) located in the Appalachian Plateau Region.

8. Coal, crushed stone, cement, and lime are some of the key products of the

   (mining, manufacturing) industry.

9. Many Virginians work for the (federal government, tourism industry) because

   Washington, D.C., sits on Virginia's northern border.

10. Virginia has become a leader in (shipbuilding, high technology) because of its connections

    with the federal government.

Notes for Home: Your child learned about some of the important industries in Virginia today and about some of the many different products made in Virginia.
Home Activity: Show your child a map of Virginia and point out the different regions and locations discussed in this lesson. Talk about these locations and some of the industries that exist there and the products that are produced.

Name _____ Date _____

 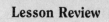
Lesson 2: Life in Modern Virginia

Directions: Answer the questions below about life in modern Virginia. You may use your textbook.

1. What are the three branches of Virginia's state government?

    _____

2. What are the duties of the three branches of Virginia's government?

    _____

    _____

    _____

    _____

3. What is the difference between income tax, sales tax, and property tax? Why do state and local governments in Virginia need to tax their residents?

    _____

    _____

    _____

    _____

    _____

4. Why are the urban areas of Virginia growing in population?

    _____

    _____

    _____

5. Who was Virginian Arthur Ashe? Why is he a good role model?

    _____

    _____

    _____

    _____

 Notes for Home: Your child learned about various aspects of life in modern Virginia.
Home Activity: Discuss the many examples of natural beauty and history that enrich the lives of Virginians and draw many people to visit Virginia.

© Scott Foresman 4 VA

Read a Time Zone Map

Directions: A time zone map shows different time zones from one region to the next. The map on this page shows the time zones in the United States. Answer the following questions on the lines provided.

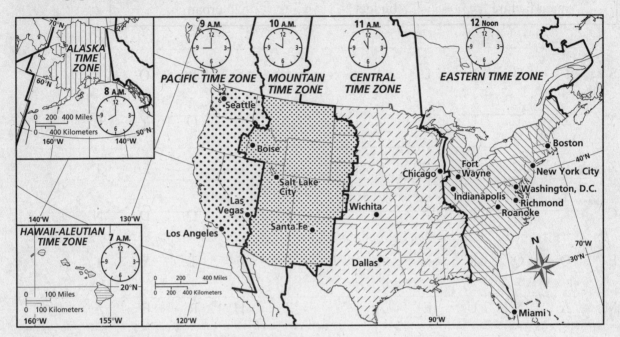

1. What are the six time zones of the United States?

_____

_____

2. In which time zone is Richmond located?

_____

3. What time is it in Salt Lake City when it is noon in Richmond?

_____

4. When it is 6 P.M. in Richmond, what time is it in Chicago?

_____

5. By how many hours is it later in the Eastern Time Zone than it is in the Pacific Time Zone?

_____

Notes for Home: Your child learned how to read a time zone map.
Home Activity: With your child, play a game in which you take turns quizzing each other about times in different cities and states in different time zones in the United States.

Name _____ Date _____

Vocabulary Review

Directions: Find and circle the vocabulary words from Chapter 13 in the word search puzzle below.

manufacture	budget	urban

```
S  I  H  L  U  A  S  H  C  R  O  V
Y  Z  T  U  R  X  E  A  B  O  Y  L
Z  D  G  U  B  F  B  U  D  G  E  T
C  E  N  S  A  A  V  E  D  D  D  N
E  Q  Q  R  N  S  J  F  E  T  Y  T
M  A  N  U  F  A  C  T  U  R  E  A
T  U  L  W  J  A  R  Z  O  A  E  T
U  L  U  Y  U  M  O  A  J  B  A  P
```

Directions: Complete the paragraph below with the three vocabulary words.

_____

My uncle Jack works in a factory where people _____

parts for ships. He works in an _____ area, but he drives a
long way home to a house in the suburbs. Jack wants to run for governor one day.
He has some terrific plans for the state. He feels he could recommend a

_____ that would please most people. He has strong ideas
about where Virginia's money should go! He's not ready to run for governor yet, so
he will keep going to his job and dreaming about the future.

Notes for Home: Your child learned the vocabulary terms for Chapter 13.
Home Activity: Take turns with your child using each of the terms in this chapter to describe some aspect
of life in modern-day Virginia.

© Scott Foresman 4 VA

Name _____ Date _____

UNIT
6 Project   Great State

Directions: In a group, create a booklet that shows what's great about Virginia today—and what will be great in the future. Then share your booklet with the class.

1. The current event in Virginia that we chose is _____.

2. Here is my paragraph about our event and a prediction of what will happen in the future:

   _____

   _____

   _____

   _____

3. Here are some ideas for a picture that I will draw or find to illustrate our event and what might occur in the future:

   _____

   _____

   _____

4. For our booklet, we will arrange our paragraphs and illustrations in this order:

   _____

   _____

   _____

✔ **Checklist for Students**

_____ We chose a current event in Virginia.

_____ We wrote paragraphs about the event and predicted what will happen in the future.

_____ We illustrated the event today and what might happen in the future.

_____ We put our group's paragraphs and pictures together in a booklet.

_____ We shared our booklet with the class.

Notes for Home: Your child helped create a booklet that summarized a current event in Virginia and showed what's great about our state.
Home Activity: With your child, discuss some other interesting or significant topics that show what's great about Virginia.